fresh fly flavor

Fab 5 Freddy

LONGMEADOW
P R E S S

To my mother, Theresa Brathwaite,
my father, Fred Brathwaite,
my sister, Nicole,
and my good friend, Emma Nine.

Published by Longmeadow Press,
201 High Ridge Road, Stamford, CT 06904

Cover and interior design by Erik Council

Original art and interior layout by Kelvin Oden

Library of Congress Cataloging-in-Publication
Data
Fab 5 Freddy.
  Fresh Fly Flavor: words and phrases of the
hip-hop generation/Fab 5 Freddy a.k.a.
Fred Brathwaite.
    p. cm.
  ISBN 0-681-41169-4
  1. Afro-American youth—Language (New words,
slang, etc.)—Dictionaries. 2. English
language—United States—Slang—
Dictionaries. 3. Black English—Dictionaries. 4.
Americanisms— Dictionaries.
  I. Title.
  PE3727.N4F3   1992
  427′.973′08996—dc20   91-30323
                                                   CIP

Printed in U.S.A.

First Edition

Repeating photo of Fab Five Freddy courtesy of MTV.

Introduction

By James Bernard

Each generation of African Americans has presented its gift to this country's musical quilt. From gospel to blues to jazz to soul to funk and, now, hip-hop, we have brought the noise to shake this country's walls to the foundation and boldly raise the roof to high heaven—really, ever since we (unhappily) first saw these shores. But the jazz era was special: it brought with it the advent of the "cool." In their zoot-suited splendor, folks like Charlie Parker, Miles Davis and John Coltrane seemed to exist in another place and time—a much *hipper* place and time—where they created a way to looking at the world that seemed other-worldly. Time itself seemed to slow down and respectfully step aside for them, as they strutted through this world.

As a young child—the son of a jazz disciple and the godson of famed percussionist Max Roach—Fab Five Freddy grew up immersed in bebop culture. He heard stories about Lester Young's saying "bread" when he meant "money." He heard Cab Calloway use "cool" when he meant "fine." And he heard many of his father's friends use "dynamite" when they meant "really, really fine." Twisting and churning the Queen's English, these jazz greats made language work for them. In their hands, it became a tool for liberation that they flaunted as defiantly as they flaunted social conventions, creating their own smoky, hep-cat world in those late night clubs where they could roam freely and shutting out the "square" world with its tight-assed artificial walls where they couldn't.

Rappers took this linguistic inventiveness one step further: they created an entire subculture based on hijacking the English language. Hip-hop culture is driven by clever wordplay and skillful delivery. Equal parts storytelling and poetry, rap tells the story of a post-Civil Rights Movement young generation, which has been afloat, lost to deteriorating communities and low self-esteem. By taking our anger and experiences and throwing them back in our faces, rap artists have empowered an entire generation, reaching young people in ways that the school system, the church and mainstream political organizations have failed. More than mere dance music, hip-hop is a cultural movement akin to the Harlem Renaissance.

When hip-hop culture came careening out of New York City's public parks, everyone thought it was a fad, that it would fizzle out with the whimper of a boom box's dying D-Cell battery. Everyone, of course, except the artists themselves and the kids who were mesmerized by the music. That sound. Those aural collages: swirling beats which boggled the mind, as well as rattled the teeth. But the real drawing cards were the lyrics, lush with double (and often triple) meanings and syncopated with asymmetrical rhythms.

The words and phrases may have been familiar but their meaning took flight on new paths. Thanks to New York rapper Busy Bee, "dope"—something that threatens to destroy our communities—became an adjective of the highest praise, a perverse reinterpretation of our reality. Refusing to fade away like yesterday's fad, hip-hop culture has grown beyond the wildest dreams of those pioneers who first plugged their turntables into park lampposts. These days, hip-hop has a voracious appetite for anything new and, along the way, has made room under its umbrella for music ranging from Public Enemy's sonic assault to Heavy D's new jack swing, from Yo-Yo hardcore womanism to Queen Latifah's R&B romance, from Digital Underground's silly but serious funk to Poor Righteous Teachers' ragga-flavor, from MC Hammer's dancing machine to Ice Cube's bass-slathered, street-isms.

Rap's passion and honesty (and, yes, its funkyness) has also attracted millions of music fans who are not Black or who don't live in urban areas. Rap fans are both male and female, and are found across all racial lines. Rap fans live in the inner city as well as the suburbs, and can be in their early or late teens just as easily as their twenties or even well into their thirties. Hip-hop—the fashion, humor, attitude and lifestyle that surround the music—is more than funky beats and clever rhymes. Hip-hop is a cultural juggernaut. Hip-hop is a way of wearing your clothes and a way of looking at the world that finds itself in the new jack swing of Guy, in house music clubs or on *In Living Color*.

Today's hepcats are the b-boys and b-girls, with their baseball caps and hooded sweatshirts or their brightly-colored kinte cloth outfits. This book is an effort to find the thread which binds rap and hip-hop in all of its many outlets: language. Our generation's quest to find our way through this sometimes hostile society can be traced through the words and phrases that we have mutated or invented. Taking up this challenge, Fab Five Freddy's glossary drives home the fact that we hip-hoppers have created a language, which underpins and drives this rich subculture. By guiding us through this myriad of new terms, Fab Five Freddy helps to facilitate understanding like an ambassador and give us a valuable reference point like Webster. As hip-hop develops faster and faster, new words and phrases stroll onto the scene everyday, and *Fresh Fly Flavor* will help you catch up and keep up. *Fresh Fly Flavor* is a report from the trenches, since Freddy—as artist, as MTV personality, as video director, as writer—has done as much to forge this culture even as he has to make sense of it. *Fresh Fly Flavor* is a guide for the uninitiated and a check point for hip-hop vets. And since his subject is changing and dynamic, expect to wrestle with it instead of merely reading it, to talk back to it instead of only letting it talk to you.

James Bernard, Senior Editor
The Source
San Francisco, February 28, 1992

CTION—Something that is going on, good, bad, or otherwise. "Yo, last night the party was jumping off. That's where the *action* was."

FROLISTIC—Introduced by the group "The Afros," known for injecting a major dose of humor and Seventies black culture into the hip-hop scene with their huge Jackson Five style afro hairdos (wigs). Afrolistic was heard on one of their songs and became a funny way of describing someone or something that would otherwise be called Afrocentric. "Listic" comes from George Clinton, the Seventies funk giant (Parliament-Funkadelics), who created many words that ended this way.

IN'T BUYING IT—1. Total disbelief. 2. Unacceptance of the way you're being treated. Lots of contemporary slang deals with business, money, or financial terms. The chief reason being that people in urban communities where 98% of all slang originates, spend a lot of time in pursuit of cash money. It's almost a subconscious way of reminding yourself that money, money, money is some important shit. So be expecting to see lots of words and phrases that remind you of money, I mean getting paid, I mean taking care of business. "Did you hear what Vanilla Ice's bio said about him growing up with the bros and being real hard? *I ain't buying it."*

IN'T GOING OUT LIKE THAT—1. Not the situation you expect to be involved in. 2. Don't like the way you're being treated "I went to work the other day to find out I was being laid off. On top of that, they say I'm not entitled to unemployment. *Well, I ain't going out like that,* 'cause I'm gonna get mines!"

IN'T HALF STEPPIN'—1. Doing the best possible job you can do. 2. Going all the way with a situation.

IN'T HAVING IT—A desire to prevent a future situation from developing, or to stop a current situation.

IN'T NO JOKE—1. Being serious. 2. A good appraisal of something. Popularized by Rakim on his record "I Ain't No Joke."

IN'T NO THANG—Not a big deal. Sometimes people even say, *"Ain't no thang but a chicken wing."*

Amazon in effect. *Photo A. Kyser*

IN'T WITH THAT—Not in agreement with the situation.

.K.'s—Abbreviation for one of the most deadly weapons: the AK-47. You'll see several other references to weapons that are favored in America's urban cities in this book, echoing the sad fact that a huge portion of black men will die violent deaths attributed to these kinds of weapons. Many of today's leading rappers including KRS-One and Chuck D. from Public Enemy make references to various types of firearms often used to kill black men. STOP THE VIOLENCE.

LL THE WAY LIVE—An extremely positive appraisal of a situation or thing. "He has a beautiful girl, a brand new car, and a college degree. That brother is definitely *all the way live."*

MAZON—A shapely woman about six feet tall, built for speed, and ready for duty.

ND ALL THAT—Derived from "all that and more." "The Geto Boys' new album is slamming, it's got dope beats, hard rhymes, *and all that."*

ND YOU KNOW THAT—Used to express agreement. "Yo, last night you had it going on, girls were treating you like a king. *And you know that."*

-BOY—Originally, B-Boy was an abbreviation for "break boy"—a totally devoted male fan and participant in hip-hop music and culture. Originally a B-Boy, like hip-hop music, was looked down upon, even by those who attended jams—the name given to parties that would spring up in parks, block parties, and community centers where hip-hop was spawned. A B-Boy was usually a feisty participant at these early jams. Here's how he got his name. When the D.J. played a record with a break beat on it, the break would start, and so would these boys. They would drop to the ground wherever they stood and perform complex foot maneuvers, twists, turns, and flips, and sometimes ended these controlled physical outbursts by spinning on their heads. They called it break dancing, and original B-Boys like Grandmaster Flash, Dynamite, and Phase II pioneered it. However, in those early days, not everyone was enthused by the B-Boy's sudden outbursts at these jams, and often looked at them with disdain, saying "Oh no, these damn B-Boys are breaking again. Don't they have any finesse?"

Many times the breaking would be competitive and sometimes lead to fighting between rival break dancing groups.

Needless to say, breaking went on to become an integral part of hip-hop culture. It had its media debut, in the early 1980s via vehicles like the motion picture "Flashdance," "Beat Street," and hip-hop's first and best film, "Wild Style."

The term B-Boy also gained popularity because, like the expression hip-hop, it was a type of reference point when describing the previous parties' highlights, as in "They started playing that hip-hop shit and them *B-Boys* started going off."

ABES—Women, girls.

ABY DOLLS—Women, girls.

ABY POP—One of the guys.

ACK IN THE DAYS—Your past. Most memorably used in KRS-One's classic "South Bronx" which also launched his career back in 1986. ***"Back in the days when hip-hop began, with Coke La Rock Kool Herc at Def Jams..."***

ACK STABBER—Someone previously trusted who turns on you.

BMW 850 Sports Car. *Photo Fab 5 Freddy*

AD—One of the oldest black expressions dating back to the 1920s and 1930s meaning: excellent, good, stylish, and cool.

ALLIN'—1. Having intercourse. 2. Playing basketball.

ASE HEAD—Someone addicted to cocaine, who free-bases it or smokes crack.

EAMER—A BMW automobile.

EAM UP—The act of smoking crack. Derived from Captain Kirk's command "Beam me up, Scotty," from the television series "Star Trek"— a metaphor for the supposed rush one gets from smoking crack.

EAT DOWN—a serious physical beating by one or more persons.

ET—An emphatic way of saying yes.

EEF—A disagreement with someone that is usually on the verge of getting violent.

ELIEVE DAT—The equivalent of telling someone it's the absolute, cross your heart and hope to die truth. "We will be getting extra busy and crazy hype at my party tonight, you can *believe dat!"*

ENZO—A Mercedes Benz.

BID—A jail sentence.

BITING (pronounced "bitin'," rhymes with "fightin'")— To copy someone.

BLASTED—Very high on drugs or alcohol.

BLEND—To incorporate yourself into a place or a situation in a smooth manner. "I've never been to this club so I'm gonna go *blend* a little and see what the flavor's like."

BLITZED—Same as blasted, if not a little higher.

BLOCK PARTY—A summer celebration common in all five boroughs of New York City, where streets are closed to traffic and music, fun, B*B*Que, and games are enjoyed by all. In rap's infancy, during the Seventies, the block party was one of the first proving grounds for many of hip-hop's pioneers. Everybody say HO! HO!

BLOW—Cocaine.

BLUNT—Marijuana rolled in an emptied out cigar wrapping.

BLOWED AWAY—1. Ovewhelmed by a situation. 2. Shot dead.

BOGART OR BOGARDE—1. To push someone around. 2. To physically control the basketball. 3. To hold on to something too long when others want it.

BOMBED—Drunk or high.

BONIN'—The act of sex.

BOOGIE—To enjoy oneself with dance and music.

BOOGIE DOWN BRONX—Bronx, New York, the birthplace of hip-hop rap music.

BOOK OR BOOKED—To leave a situation or place, "I thought Gang Starr was on the Wild Pitch label, but they *booked* and went to Chrysalis for a better deal."

BOOMIN' SYSTEM—1. Loud, powerful stereo system installed in a car. 2. A shapely woman.

BOOSTIN'—Shoplifting.

OX—A portable stereo cassette/radio.

REAK IT DOWN—1. To further explain. 2. The change of the flow in a piece of music. "The beat was flowing along kinda like this—boom pap pap boom pap, boom pap pap boom pap. Then came the *break down*—ta ta ta ta ta ta ta ta, boom pap pap boom pap . . ."

REAK BEAT—1. Song containing an instrumental drum dominated section, ideal for the purpose of making hip-hop music. Let me explain. In the beginning days of hip-hop, long before the idea of making records and fortunes was even a dream, the key ingredients for being involved were: some sort of sound system, hopefully, two working turntables, various indispensable records like Chic's "Goodtimes," M.F.S.B.'s "Love is the Message," and Apache's "Bongo Rock"—in pairs of course—a mixer to segue back and forth between the two records, and an M.C./rapper to talk up a blue streak on the microphone. Now, with all these ingredients in place and functioning, to go to the highest heights, each area needs to be constantly improved on—equipment wise, record wise, and rapper wise.

The break beats are of chief importance to the D.J. so he must hunt relentlessly for new and improved pieces of music to cut up, scratch, and mix for his rapper. The introduction of compilation records (you guessed it, they were called break beat records) containing all the common break beats used by hip-hop's pioneering D.J.s like Kool Herc, made the process easier for all involved in the early 1980s. Herc pioneered the use of the break beat and introduced one of the most popular break beats—Apache's "Bongo Rock."

REAK ASS—To cause someone serious bodily harm.

REAKOUT—To leave with haste. Similar to "Booked" but a little quicker.

REW—Beer or malt liquor.

UCKIN'—Shooting a weapon.

UCKS—Money.

UCK WILD—To act rambunctious and aggressive. "They had a wild party after the step show and the boys were acting *buck wild,* like something outta 'Animal House.' "

UGGIN'—Derived from "buggin' out." Buggin' can be anything from complete irrational behavior like walking nude through Times Square, to playful behavior like tossing fully-clothed, unsuspecting friends into swimming pools.

UMPIN'—1. Good. 2. Good, throbbing, funky music." The party was jumpin', the music was bumpin'."

UM RUSH—To forcefully enter when not invited. "So after trying to reach him by phone for six months and his secretary constantly giving me the runaround, me and a posse of five jumped out of a jeep, stormed in and **bum rushed** his office." Also, the title of Public Enemy's 1988 debut album, "Yo! Bum Rush the Show!"

URNED—1. To be cheated. 2. To catch a venereal disease.

UST—To do something.

UST A CAP—To shoot a gun, also same as "buckin'."

UST THE MOVE OR BUS IT—Check this out.

UST YOU OUT—To have sex.

USTED—1. Arrested. 2. Caught doing something wrong.

ALI—California

ADDY—Cadillac.

ALL YOU OUT—Asking someone to fight.

AN YOU RELATE—Can you understand?

APPIN'—Shooting guns. The origin of the term is the expression "I'll bust a cap in your ass." This is usually what you tell somebody you're not quite pleased with. However, going back even farther, the origin is the cap pistols most little boys played with.

AN'T HANG—Not fun to be around. Also means has no particular ability to do something, like play basketball, drink alcohol, dance, whatever.

HEEBA—Originally a potent form of marijuana. Now just a generic term for it. Rhymes with amoeba (you know, a one-celled animal). Marijuana.

HILL—Relax.

HOCOLATE CITY—Washington, D.C., which is predominantly black.

HOWIN' DOWN—Eating food.

HUMP—A weak, scared, or timid individual in the eyes of those who are otherwise.

LEAN—To be well-dressed. *"Clean as the Board of Health."*

LOCKIN'—1. To watch someone intently. 2. To admire with a sexual desire. 3. To accumulate large sums of money. "Yo, every week Daddy's House is packed, I know they're *clockin'* crazy dollars."

LOUT—Having connections and influence.

-LOW—A dice game popular in New York City using three dice.

LUCKER—A person addicted to smoking crack.

.O.—Correction officer.

OLD—1. Derived from cold blooded. Cool, attractive, stylish. 2. Extreme.

OLD BLOODED—No emotion.

OLD CHILLIN'—Totally relaxed. (Also, a popular rap record label.)

OLD STEEL—A knife or a gun.

OLORS—1. Proof of belonging in a gang in the form of jackets with the gangs' names across the back. 2. Red or blue, the colors that represent the Bloods and Crips, California's two largest gangs.

OME CORRECT—1. To execute a situation exactly. 2. To tell the truth.

OME OFF—Appear.

OOKIN'—1. A social gathering that people are enjoying. "Parties at L.L. Cool J.'s hour are always cookin'." 2. Something you like that's attractive or stylish. "She drove off in a 560 drop-top Benz with the spoiler-kit, and lookin' like home **cookin'**." 3. Excellent.

OOL—1. A form of approval. "Big Daddy Kane is one *cool* brother. 2. A mellow, relaxed attitude. You know, cool is one of the oldest and most used slang expressions. The word dates back to the early 1930s and was popularized by jazz musicians who often described each other, when

applicable, as "cool cats." Cats, being naturally mellow and relaxed animals, became a symbol for a generation of hipsters who also referred to each other as cats, as in: "A couple of **cats** stopped by the club for a jam session last night. It was really **cool**."

Of course, the other obvious reference is when the temperature drops below 32°. At that point, things can be termed "cool as ice," meaning the same as above: mellow, relaxed, and just plain cool. Other offshoots of the term cool can be seen in previous entries: cold blooded, cold chillin', and cold steel.

OOLIN' OUT—The act of resting or relaxing.

OP—1. To go buy something.

OP AN ATTITUDE—To get upset.

OP A PLEA—To beg forgiveness in a bad situation.

OP OUT—To remove yourself from a situation. "Not finishing college because you don't like the color of the cafeteria is a total **cop out**."

RACK—A form of cocaine obtained after a chemical process which results in an extremely potent, highly addictive drug.

RACKIN' ON YOU—To talk negatively about you in a humorous manner.

RANK—A combination of crack cocaine and amphetamines.

RASH—1. To go to sleep. 2. The tired, down feeling one has after doing illegal drugs.

RAZY—see "mad."

RAZY LARGE—1. Doing extremely well. 2. Having success. 3. Having lots of money.

REW—1. Your immediate group of close friends. 2. The people who travel with a D.J. or rapper.

REEPIN'—To move slowly and cautiously.

RIB—Home.

Early Hip Party at Celebrity Club. At turntable is Love Bug
Starsky, Busy Bee and Grand Master Caz. *Photo Charlie Ahearn*

ROOKLAND—Used to describe the dangerous areas of Brooklyn, New York.

RUISIN'—Driving around slowly.

RUMB SNATCHERS—Little children.

UT—1. To dilute illegal drugs. 2. To manually manipulate one or two records on a turntable to create a percussive sound in time to the beat. Cutting is one of the building blocks in the hip-hop structure and dates back to its origins. Grandmaster Flash, in the early 1970s, was the first to actually use the technique of cutting a record as a then aspiring D.J.

Two copies of the same record or two different records can be used. The basic idea is not so much cutting but intercutting the two records together to, in some cases, create a remixed version of the record.

The key aspect is to never miss a beat so everything flows like water in the Nile. The desired effect is to have you rockin' to a slammin' beat that you may be familiar with and then suddenly, whammo, you hear one fragment of another part of the same record drop down without interrupting the flow. "Flash will *cut* the record down to the bone."

UT ME SOME SLACK—The same as give me a break.

AP—1. To be well dressed. 2. Slapping someone's palms to show agreement. Also known as giving some skin and slapping five, **i.e.**, two friends or acquaintances, usually male, who see each other and slap each other's hands as a form of greeting, or to show agreement.

AYTONS—Expensive car tire rims, sought after by thieves.

EAD PRESIDENTS—An old-school hustlers' expression for American money, obviously referring to the pictures of old white men who adorn each bill's face. This expression was revitalized by the master rapper Rakim on his record "Paid in Full": " . . . so I start my mission, leave my residence, thinking how I could get some *dead presidents . . . "*

EAL WITH IT—To handle and adjust to a situation or thing.

EALIN'—The act of selling drugs.

EEP SIX—Murder, "He was a nice guy, but got *deep sixed* by the mob." The term refers to the act of being killed and buried.

EF—A high form of praise. However, the term was originally pronounced "death" but constant usage caused its evolution to the current pronunciation. Def, like dope and bad—the granddaddy of slang expressions —is an example of the way urban black English has made the negative seem positive or made that which is unpopular in the eyes of mass culture, popular in the eyes of underground culture.

EUCE AND A QUARTER—A Buick Electra 225.

IME—Ten dollars.

ISS—To disrespect. "Nobody disses me and gets away with it."

Doe, paper, cash money, dead presidents, etc. *Photo David Merrill*

IVIDENDS—Money.

.J.—Disc jockey, radio, or party. 2. In dance-hall reggae, the rapper is referred to as the "D.J." and the "selector" is the one who plays the recording.

OG—To treat badly.

OG YOU OUT—Talk about you in a negative way.

OGS—Feet.

O DAMAGE—1. Doing something well, **i.e.** when an M.C. like Lord Finesse rocks the mike it's called *"doing damage"* 'cause he's so good. 2. Having sex.

O-OR-DIE-BED STUY—The Bedford-Stuyvesant section of Brooklyn, and my birthplace.

O WORK—Doing a good, thorough job. "The crowd was like going crazy screaming and carrying on, so we stepped on stage and commenced to *do work.*"

O YOU UP—To have sexual intercourse.

OIN' IT or **DOIN' THE DO**—Having sexual intercourse.

ON'T BELIEVE THE HYPE—Introduced by Public Enemy: Don't believe everything you read, see, or hear in the media.

ON'T EVEN TRY IT—Don't give it any consideration or thought.

ON'T FESS—1. Don't go back on your word. 2. Don't start what you can't finish.

ON'T WRITE A CHECK YOUR ASS CAN'T CASH—Don't say you can do what you're not capable of.

ON'T SWEAT ME—1. Don't nag. 2. Don't try to be involved in my life.

OOBIE—A marijuana cigarette or joint.

OOKIE—Describes something big, usually jewelry. "Kimyatta always wears those fat, *dookie* gold earrings."

20

Busy Bee on mike, Cool D.J. A.J. on turntable at Ecstasy Garage, Bronx, NY. *Photo Charlie Ahearn*

OPE—A high form of praise, as in excellent. Dope is one of hip-hop's most commonly used expressions and was introduced around the mid-1980s by one of rap's pioneers, the Chief Rocker Busy Bee. I remember first hearing him use it at a New Music Seminar Rap Battle as Melle Mel, a member of Grand Master Flash and the Furious Five M.C.s, was about to take part. "Yo Mel, kick that *dope* shit, homeboy. Let me see you get busy."

I was sitting right in front of Busy, who was also accompanied by Water Bed Kevie-Kev from the legendary rap group from the old school, Grand Wizard Theodore and the Fantastic Five M.C.s.

Kev was also encouraging Mel by telling him to say something dope. I remember the complex feeling I had when I heard that word used in such an obviously radical fashion. You know, one of society's ultimate definitions of wrong-doing was being elevated to a quasi-positive meaning. An extension of bad, when used in the black sense, of course, is what the complete acceptance of this word means.

Its common usage also reminds us that a key ingredient in ultra urban, contemporary counter-youth-culture is to flirt with what's wrong, take the negative vibe and power, and turn it all the way around to make it serve a new purpose, yet with the shock value still intact.

DOUBLE DEUCE—A twenty-two caliber pistol.

DOUGH—Money.

DOWN—1. To get closely involved with a person or a situation. 2. To be in agreement, "The money's right, the people seem cool, I'd love to be **down** with this situation."

DOWN BY LAW—Officially involved in a situation as decreed by someone in charge as in crew, posse, or employer. "I started out as a fan until Chuck D. made me part of the crew with a salary and all, now I'm **down by law."**

DOWN FOR THE COUNT—1. Not able to finish an endeavor. 2. Knocked out in a fight. 3. Sleeping.

DREADLOCKS—The hairstyle synonymous with those involved in the Rastafarian religion and culture. The style is typified by the long, matted intertwined locks of hair that occur naturally when kinky hair is allowed to grow without brushing or combing.

Bob Marley. *Photo Adrian Boot. Courtesy of Island Records*

Bob Marley, the world's most noted wearer of dreadlocks.
Photo Adrian Boot. Courtesy of Island Records

The world's most noted wearer of this style was the late, great musical legend Bob Marley who made the dreadlock style and reggae music a familiar part of world culture.

RESSED TO KILL—Dressed to impress with the finest in current fashion.

RIVE BY—A West coast gang style shooting that occurs from a passing automobile.

ROP A BOMB—To tell someone a surprising and enlightening fact.

ROP A DIME—To turn someone in to the police.

ROP SCIENCE—To inform, explain, and educate in a knowledgable fashion. The phrase was popularized by the *Five Per-centers*.

ROP TOP—A convertible automobile.

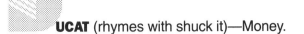

UCAT (rhymes with shuck it)—Money.

IGHT BALL—Olde English 800 malt liquor, an extremely popular beverage among hip-hoppers, frequently referred to in numerous rap songs as a 40 ounce.

NDS—Money.

XTRA LARGE—1. Living well. 2. Very successful.

ADE—Type of hairstyle where the hair is lower on the sides than it is on top.

AKE THE MOVE—Appearing to do one thing while actually doing another.

ALL-IN—To join the activities.

AT—Living well, doing well, being successful.

ELL OFF—A person who's no longer involved or doing well as in any rapper who's started smoking crack and making poor records—he *fell off.*

ESS UP—Tell the truth.

IGHT THE POWER—Fight the system that oppresses you.

IVE PERCENTER—An Islamic organization based in New York City, with many rappers as members including Rakim, King Sun, Brand Nubians, Poor Righteous Teachers, and Lakim Shabazz. This group was started by Clarence 13X when he became disenchanted with the teachings of Elijah Muhammad. They believe that the Asiatic black man is God. They often refer to one another as God. A greeting used is "Peace God."

IRED UP—1. To be angry at someone or thing. 2. The act of getting high on drugs or alcohol.

IVE-O—Police.

LAVOR—1. The tone or vibe of a person, place or situation. 2. Something good. 3. The name of one of hip-hop's most colorful stars, Flavor Flav from the group, Public Enemy.

LEX—To act like you want trouble.

LICK—Movie.

A bunch of girls looking fly. *Photo A. Kyser*

LIPPED—1. Gone crazy. 2. Got very upset.

LIPPIN'—1. Acting wild. 2. Very upset.

LUNKY—A person eager to do anything for a person who doesn't appreciate it.

LY—High form of praise. Fly dates back to an expression commonly used in the 1960s, "superfly." This expression usually described how you looked when dressed in your flashiest threads and were about to party.

In the 1970s when black action movies were hot, a film was made entitled "Superfly," which was the story of a renegade coke dealer trying to make lots of money and get out of the business.

Hip-hoppers picked up the term in the mid-1970s and chiefly used it to describe well-dressed, avid female rap fans as "fly girls." By the early 80s, "fly girls" as an expression faded out, but the fly part stayed and gained new life as one of this generation's most complimentary words. "I liked the way you handled that situation, it was very *fly*."

REAK—A wild, sexually active person.

The Fantastic 5 M.C.s, originators of the term "fresh." *Photo Charlie Ahearn*

REAKED OUT—1. Startled and upset by a sudden occurrence. 2. The aftermath of a sexual encounter with a freak.

REE STYLE—1. To perform not according to plan. 2. To execute a performance or dance of any kind with total improvisation. 3. To say rhymes off the top of your head a capella or to a funky hip-hop break beat, i.e., during a rap concert where a popular artist is performing some material that's never been recorded with a much looser, free style.

RESH—Originated by one of hip-hop's original groups who never received wide notoriety. They were originally called Grand Wizard Theodore and the Fantastic 5 M.C.s, who later changed their name to the Fantastic Freaks. A part of their performance routine was to say: "We're *fresh* out the pack so you gotta stay back, we got one Puerto Rican and the rest are black."

When talking to their peers and fans they would always describe that at their next jam (party) they would be performing new material that would be *"fresh* out the pack."

Obviously, they liked the expression, which has been shortened to fresh, and is perhaps the ultimate positive assessment and appraisal of anything.

ROM THE GIT GO or **FROM THE GITTY-UP**—From the beginning.

RONTIN'—1. Trying to impress someone. 2. Telling lies.

ULL EFFECT—To be at your fullest and your presence is seen, heard, and felt, i.e., when a situation is revealed after careful planning and preparation you can say it's now in *full effect*.

UNKY OR FONKY—1. A state of mind, music, clothes, or attitude that can come from being totally immersed in black music and culture. 2. All that which derives from the funk master, the Godfather of Soul, the Hardest Working Man in Show Business, Mr. Dynamite—James Brown.

OUR ONE ONE/411—News and information. "I heard there was a riot in Bensonhurst after the Stop the Violence demonstration. So who's got the *411* on the situation?"

ANG BANGIN'—The act of being in and involved with a street gang, particularly those on the West Coast.

AS FACE—Popularized by the group 3rd Bass in their song of the same title. The expression defines a silly look one could possibly make when wanting to express extreme displeasure with someone or something.

ET A GRIP—To gain control of any situation or occurrence.

ET A LIFE—To get one's act together.

ET BOMBED—To become very high on drugs or alcohol.

ET BUSY—To start doing something.

ET DONE—1. To be shot. 2. Have sex.

ET DOWN—1. To start something. 2. Have sex. 3. Play music hard and well. 4. Party hard.

ET DUMB—Act crazy or wild.

ET IT TOGETHER—1. To pull oneself together. 2. To do it well.

ET LAID—Have sex.

ET LOOSE—To have fun.

ET NICE—Get high.

ET OFF—Sexual orgasm.

ET OVER—1. To obtain a goal. 2. To trick someone.

ET PLAYED—To be embarrassingly deceived or taken advantage of.

ET STUPID—1. To act silly. 2. To have a raucous good time. This term was first popularized by rap artist Joeski Love on his mid-1980s classic "Pee Wee's Dance." i.e. "Everybody was *getting real stupid* at Davy-D's Hip-Hop Halloween party last night."

ET WITH THE PROGRAM—To get involved. This term is usually used when one feels that another should understand and be involved in a certain situation.

HETTO BLASTER—A sizable portable stereo system.

IG—A job.

O FOR BROKE—1. To perform at one's fullest in pursuit of one's goals. 2. One's last all-out attempt.

O WITH THE FLOW—To smoothly involve yourself in a situation or relationship without causing any problems. "Don't make trouble at your new job, just *go with the flow*."

OOD TO GO—Everything is fine and ready.

OING OUT LIKE A SUCKER—1. To be obviously taken advantage of by someone. 2. To make a fool of one's self.

OT IT GOING ON—Doing well, living well, being successful.

OT IT LIKE THAT—1. An abundance of something good. 2. That's how it is.

OT PULL—Clout.

OT YOU COVERED—Everything will be taken care of. *"Got you covered* like a rug."

OT YOUR BACK—Looking out for someone's interest, physical or otherwise.

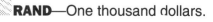

RAND—One thousand dollars.

30

RILL—Face.

ROOVE, TO BE IN THE—To be mentally and/or spiritually in sync.

ROOVY—A pleasantly flowing situation.

UMBY (haircut)—Originally, the name of a popular animated clay figure who had a lopsided head and a T.V. show in the '60s and '70s. However, Bobby Brown, the current New Jack R&B artist made the hairstyle popular. The hair is cut higher on one side than the other and low around the sides.

ANDLING THINGS—The situation is under control.

ANG OUT—1. To socialize with friends. 2. To enjoy oneself with one's friends.

ARD—1. Mean and ruthless. 2. A positive appraisal, usually addressing music or attitude.

AWK—A brisk cold wind.

EMMED UP—To physically assault or detain.

IGH ROLLER—Someone making and spending big money, usually involved with illegal activities.

IGH-FIVE—To slap hands vigor-ously high above the head to show agree-ment or approval of a thing or situation.

IP—1. To know the ins and outs of what's going on around you. 2. To be attuned to street culture.

IP-HOP—1. The term originated in the mid-1970s during the beginning stages of what is also known as rap. It was first said by D.J. Hollywood, who, while playing records, would get on the mike and shout: "To the *hip-hop* the hippy hippy hippy hippy hop and you don't stop."

This caught on and other pioneering D.J.s & M.C.s in Harlem and the Bronx picked up on it. It became the one expression used by everyone involved. Fans, when explaining the previous night's party experiences, would use the word hip-hop to describe and identify what type of party it was. The term is now used to specify the type of rap music that is close and true to the original attitude. 2. Style and state of mind as established by the originators of hip-hop music and culture.

IP-HOUSE—Rap lyrics laid down over house music (see House Music).

IT—A Mafia-type killing.

IT IT—Start the music.

IT MAN—A paid assassin.

OE-HOPPIN'—To have sex with numerous promiscuous women.

OMEBOY—A male from your place of origin or hometown.

OMEGIRL—A female from your place of origin or hometown.

OMES—1. An acquaintance from your home town. 2. A way of addressing someone when you don't really know their name.

OMEY—Same as above.

OMEY DON'T PLAY THAT—I don't agree with the situation. Phrase popularized by Damon Wayans' character Homey the Clown on the TV show "In Living Color."

ONEYS—Attractive young girls.

OOD—1. The neighborhood where you live. 2. A gangster.

OOKED—1. To have something totally controlled. 2. To be addicted to drugs.

OOK YOU UP—To take care of something for another.

OOPTIE—A beat-up, broken-down car still running and somewhat appreciated.

OTTIE—A sexy young girl.

OUSE—To attack someone violently.

OUSE MUSIC—Monotonous, droning, fast tempo dance music which emerged from Chicago in the late 1980s. (Ugh!)

OW YA LIVIN'?—How are you doing/feeling?

HYPE

—1.To overly build up and exaggerate.
2.Also means something is really good.

AIN'T GOIN' FOR IT—It's intolerable.

AIN'T THE ONE—I'm not to be bothered.

CAN HANG—1. I'm capable of doing the job. 2. I can go.

CE—1. Cool. 2. A name used by numerous rappers such as Ice-T, Ice Cube, Ice Cream-T and Smooth Ice.

CED—Killed.

DON'T PLAY THAT—I don't like that.

LIKE THE WAY IT'S GOING DOWN—I like the feeling.

LLIN'—Acting wild and crazy.

'M DOWN—I'm ready.

'M OUT—I'm leaving.

'M OUTTIE 5000—I'm leaving. Derived from the name of the car Audi 5000 and popularized by the group EPMD (Eric and Parish Making Dollars).

'M STRAIGHT—1. I'm satisfied. 2. I'm off drugs. *"I'm straight* as six o'clock."

'M WITH THAT—I agree.

N A HEART BEAT—In a moment's notice.

N IT TO WIN IT—Trying your best to succeed at any endeavor or situation you're involved with.

N THE HOUSE—At the party.

N THE MIX—Involved in the situation.

PEEPED IT—I saw it.

T'S ALL THAT—High form of praise.

ACKED— A term popular on the West Coast that describes being robbed or assaulted. "I came out of the movies and realized I was jacked for my Daytons."

AM—1. A record. 2. A party where hip-hop music is played. 3. In trouble.

AMMIN'—1. Partying to hip-hop music. 2. Making good music.

AMMY—A firearm.

ERRY JUICE—The liquid substance that's used to chemically treat black hair to create waves and curls, that drips and stains clothes and bedding.

ET—To leave.

IMBROWSKI—Male sex organ.

IMMY—Male sex organ.

IMMY HAT—Condom.

INGLIN'—Originated by L.L. Cool J on the song "Jingling Baby." The term refers to the movement of women's breasts or earrings while dancing or having sex.

IVE—1. Nonsense. 2. Slang.

OCKIN'—1. To persistently and shamelessly try to emulate someone or be

37

Kimyatta in her extra fat Dookie gold earrings. *Photo A. Kyser*

involved in their life. 2. Also a term used to describe members of the opposite sex whose pursuits or advances are not wanted. "This very wack guy at school is *jockin'* me real hard and I hate it."

OINT—1. Jail. 2. Marijuana cigarette. 3. A place.

UGGLIN'—Handling several things or situations at once.

UICE—Clout.

UMBO—A large bottle of crack cocaine.

ANGOL—A brand of hat favored by many hip-hop fans and practitioners since the beginning. Currently popular on the Jamaican music scene.

ICK BACK—To relax.

ICK GAME—To try to win a woman's confidence.

ICK IT—To start.

ICK IT LIVE—To do it well.

IT—Extra body parts for a car which enhance its style and increase its appeal and speed.

NOCKIN' BOOTS—Sexual intercourse.

NOT—Fat wad of money.

NOW WHAT I'M SAYING?—Do you understand me?

NUCKLEHEAD—Stupid person.

AID BACK—1. Cool, calm, and rested. 2. Easy-going style.

ARGE—Doing well (see also *living large*).

ARGE AND IN CHARGE—Doing well and in total control.

AY IT ON ME—1. Give it to me. 2. Tell me about it.

EAVE ME HANGING—Not to slap one's hand in agreement when offered.

ET YOU SLIDE—Give you another chance.

ET'S GET IT ON—1. Start. 2. Let's have sex.

IGHTEN UP—Take it easy.

IVING FOUL—Negative ways and lifestyle.

IVING LARGE—A very popular expression in the hip-hop community which originated and gained popularity during the last few years. It began as a greeting/question: "Yo, how ya living?" The usual answer being: "Large" or "Large and in charge." Living large then became a perfect way to describe wealth, prestige, success, or all three. "Russell Simmons, the owner of Def Jam records, RUSH Productions, and several other companies is definitely *living large.*"

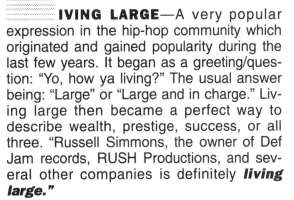

OC—Loco, crazy.

OUNGIN'—Relaxing.

OW PRO—Low profile.

ACKIN' (rhymes with packin')—1. A flamboyant life style supported by women. 2. Being in control of a situation with your wit as the chief tool.

The origin of the term goes back to the 18th century British movement called Dandyism. Dandies were usually very intelligent, quick witted—and obsessed with their dress and appearance to a point never displayed by men before. They would spend more time grooming, primping, and styling themselves than women of royalty. Oftentimes, kings, counts, and dukes would consult with them on their personal fashion needs.

British dandies were called the macaronis. The term crossed the ocean by the time of the Revolutionary War, and appeared in the song "Yankee Doodle." Macaroni was picked up by black pimps in the late 1950s who shortened it and began to refer to each other as macks or mack men to give a more prestigious air to the life style they chose. Nowadays, the term's meaning has been broadened and somewhat softened by its current popular usage in the hip-hop world. Once again, a word or phrase has been snatched up by ultra-urban contemporary black youth, re-formed, and spit back out into mainstream culture.

ACK 10—Deadly automatic weapon preferred by drug dealers and gang members.

AD—Used to describe an abundance of something. "Afrika Bambaataa, has *mad* records in his collection."

AKIN' G'S—Earning thousands of dollars.

AN, THE—Police

AXIN' AND RELAXIN'—Being cool, calm, and collected.

AX OUT—To relax.

.C.—1. Master of ceremonies. 2. One who raps hip-hop music to the funky

Slick Rick, the story teller. *Photo Def Jam Recordings/*
Columbia Records

Big Daddy Kane, smooth yet hard.
Photo Buckmaster. Cold Chillin'/Reprise

Ice Cube, West Coast Gangster Style. *Photo courtesy of Priority Records*

Money Makin' Manhattan. *Photo Fab 5 Freddy*

beat, **i.e.**, KRS-One, Ice Cube, Big Daddy Kane, Kool G. Rap, etc.

ICKEY D'S.—McDonald's fast food restaurants.

ISS THANG—A conceited woman, popularized by Black gay men.

OJO—To put a spell on somebody.

ONEY MAKIN' MANHATTAN—New York City.

UNCHIES—Craving for food after smoking marijuana.

ARC—Police who specialize in narcotics law enforcement.

EW JACK—A person new to a situation making an attempt at being the best.

EW JACK SWING—A type of R&B music with a strong street feeling added to give, at times, a hip-hop feel. The term was coined by Barry Michael Cooper.

Teddy Riley, the extremely talented producer of numerous pop, rap, and R&B artists is credited with pioneering the style. Songs that he has written, produced, or both that define the New Jack Style include: Bobby Brown's "My Prerogative," Heavy D's "We've Got Our Own Thing," and "New Jack Swing" for the rap group Wrecks in Effect that includes his little brother. He is also the leader of Guy, his own group, which was featured on the sound track for the movie "New Jack City," the story of a Harlem drug dealer brought down by a hip-hop undercover cop. Also, I must shamelessly add that yours truly was the associate producer.

EW SCHOOL—1. New artists like Cypress Hill, Brand Nubian and Leaders of The New School, with new ideas making an impact on hip-hop music. 2. The current state of mind and action of people making hip-hop music.

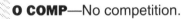

O COMP—No competition.

AKTOWN—Oakland, California.

KIE, DOKIE, THE—A type of con whre you end up being conned out of your money or personal possessions.

LD E.—Olde English 800 Malt Liquor.

N—A very flattering form of praise."The lyrics on the Brand Nubian album are definitely *on.*"

N A MISSION—Determined.

N THE DOWN LOW—Keeping a low profile, a.k.a. on the D.L.

N THE FLIP FLOP—Later on.

N THE FLIP SIDE—1. Tomorrow. 2. The other version of the story. 3. The B-side of a record.

N THE PIPE—Addicted to smoking crack.

N THE REAL SIDE—1. Truthfully. 2. For real.

N THE REBOUND—See you later.

N THE SMART TIP—See *Cool*.

N THE SMOOTH TIP—Mellow person or situation.

N THE STRENGTH—To really mean it.

N THE UP AND UP—See *On the real side*.

N TIME—The right thing at the right time, "I was hot and thirsty after work and my girl hit me with an ice cold lemonade."

UT BOX—From the beginning.

.Z.—An ounce of marijuana or some other illegal drug. It's interesting to note that there are tendencies to use initials, yet there is no specific reason why, other than some very cool, influential hipster starts and others join in until the original word is not as cool anymore.

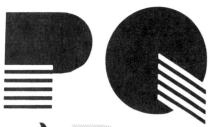

ACKIN'—Carrying a firearm.

ACKIN' A NINE—Carrying a 9mm handgun.

AID IN FULL—Popularized by the legendary rapper Rakim on his song of the same title. The term means to get the maximum money from your endeavors.

APER—Money.

APER THIN—Phony; meaning you can see through a person's actions into their true motives.

EACE—A final greeting as you depart.

EEP, PEEPING IT OUT—To look closely at a situation, person, or thing.

ERPETRATE—To profess to be what you aren't.

IECE—A handgun.

ILL, THE—A basketball.

LAY IT OFF—Act as if nothing is affecting or bothering you when it really is.

LAY ME CLOSE—see *Jockin'*.

LAY THE DOZENS—To talk humorously about each other's mother and family.

LAYED—To be taken advantage of, cheated, or conned.

LAYED LIKE A SUCKER—Being made to look stupid.

LAYED OUT—Out of style.

LAYED YOURSELF—1. To make a stupid mistake. 2. To embarrass yourself in front of others. This phrase was the title of a song released off of Ice-T's album, "The Ice Berg." "So you give her a brand new car, jewelry, and lots of expensive clothes, and she's screwing your best friend. You *played yourself.*"

LAYER—1. One who earns a living by getting all of his money from women. 2. One who earns an illegal living by using his or her wits.

OCKETS ARE FAT—Having lots of money on you. "I just got paid and my *pockets are fat.*" Same as pockets are swollen.

OINT BLANK—Absolutely.

OISON—Popularized by the group B.B.D. (Bell, Biv, Devoe) in their song of the same title. The word describes an attractive, promiscuous female.

OONTANG—1. Female sex organ 2. Sex.

OOT-BUT—A lackadaisical, unmotivated, dumb person.

OPPED—Arrested.

OSSE—A group of people that you travel with, hang out with, and who will look out for you if trouble arrives.

RIMO—A joint of marijuana laced with cocaine.

ROFILIN'—Trying to attract attention to yourself. This is usually something a mack might do. However, many do it just trying to show off or bring attention to themselves. "Did you see the guy there *profilin'* with the bright yellow polka dot track suit standing in front of the Apollo Theater with his nose in the air?"

SYCH—To fool people.

UB—Publicity.

ULL—1. Clout. 2. To win the affection and confidence of a woman.

Bel, Biv, DeVoe looking for Poison. *Photo David Roth. Courtesy of MCA Records*

UMP IT UP—1. Turn up the volume. 2. An expression sometimes chanted at parties.

UNK—An easily manipulated individual.

UT HEADS TO BED—Knocking people out.

UT UP OR SHUT UP—Give up the money promised or stop talking about it.

UT YOUR HEAD OUT—To kill someone.

.T.—1. A quarter. 2. Quiet.

UICK, FAST, AND IN A HURRY—Rapidly.

UIET AS IT'S KEPT—1. A little-known fact that should be kept that way. 2. Said of something that is obvious and well-known, but is dealt with in a clandestine manner.

AG TOP—A vehicle with synthetic fabric covering.

AINCOAT—Condom.

AP MUSIC—Poetry or rhymes set to throbbing, funk rhythm patterns. Rap music is the generic term that describes the most dominant youth music in America since the early days of rock and roll. News, views, and attitudes make up a small part of what rap music is all about. It's really about a voice that, for the most part, shouts as one what's on the mind of America's ultra urban, contemporary, vanguard black youth.

Rap music, to paraphrase Chuck D., is the Cable News Network (CNN) of the ghettoes of America. From the first rap record to hit the streets in the late 1970s, by King Tim the Third, to the current vocal gymnastics of groups like Brand Nubian, millions of words have sailed along major beats to provide the loudest voice a black man has ever had in this country and it continues to grow. (See definition of hip-hop to get the complete picture.)

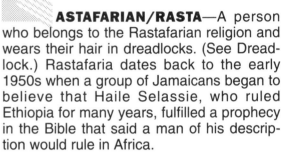

ASTAFARIAN/RASTA—A person who belongs to the Rastafarian religion and wears their hair in dreadlocks. (See Dreadlock.) Rastafaria dates back to the early 1950s when a group of Jamaicans began to believe that Haile Selassie, who ruled Ethiopia for many years, fulfilled a prophecy in the Bible that said a man of his description would rule in Africa.

When Haile Selassie visited Jamaica in the 1960s, thousands came out to greet him. This visit solidified their belief that he was earth's rightful ruler. Ras Tafari was what Selassie was called early in his life, hence the term "rastafarian." (See also reggae.)

AW—Hard, direct, truthful, and uncensored.

EAL DEAL—The absolute facts.

EAL DEAL, THE—1. The truth. 2. The way it's supposed to be..

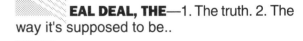

ED, BLACK, AND GREEN—The colors of black liberation worldwide; originated

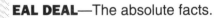

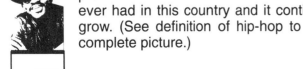

by Marcus Garvey. Black for the people, red for the blood, and green for the land.

ED BONE—A light-skinned black woman.

EGGAE—Music originated in Jamaica and widely popularized by Bob Marley and the Wailers. The sound of reggae is usually identified by its mid-tempo bass, drum-dominated rhythms, and lyrics which run the gamut from righteous upliftment to slackness—the Jamaican term for songs with x-rated lyrics.

Today, reggae music is divided into three basic categories: 1. Classical, which would include artists such as Bob Marley and the Wailers, Burning Spear, Third World, and Steel Pulse; 2. Reggae singers, which would include artists like Dennis Brown, Gregory Isaacs, Freddie McGregor, and Barrington Levy. There are also Sing J.'s, who combine singing with a rap flavor like Pinchers, Eek-a-Mouse, Coca Tea; 3. Dancehall reggae which is the hottest form of the music right now. Dancehall is the Jamaican equivalent of hip-hop. It developed in the early 1970s (as did hip-hop) from mobile sound systems that crossed Jamaica playing instrumental dub (a remixed record with extra added bass and effects) that provided the perfect foundation for the development of many talented Jamaican rappers and D.J.s. Some of the top dancehall artists include: Ninja Man, Josie Wales, Papa San, and Shabba Ranks (who collaborated with hip-hop giant

Dance Hall King Shabba Ranks. *Photo Gerhard Jurkovic. Courtesy of Epic Records*

KRS-One on a song produced by him on his debut album "Raw As Ever" on the Epic/Sony Music label.)

IDE—An automobile.

IFF—A disagreement with someone.

OCK THE SPOT—1. To give a good performance. 2. Have good sex.

OCK YOUR WORLD—1. To totally surprise or astonish. 2. Sexual intercourse.

OLL ON—To approach someone with the intent to do harm. "Lets *roll on* those suckers and kick some motherfucking ass."

OLL OUT—To leave.

OLL UP—To arrive.

OLLIN'—Making lots of money.

OSCOE—Handgun.

Dance Hall Don Papa San. *Photo courtesy of Pow Wow Records*

OACH—1. A person with no money. 2. Last portion of a marijuana cigarette.

OCK—1. A basketball. 2. Cocaine or crack in its solid form.

AME OLD SAME OLD—Unchanged.

AMPLING—To digitally record a portion of an existing record or sound and later incorporate it into a hip-hop record. This relatively recent technological advance allows up to five or more samples of music or any sound to be recorded without any loss in sound quality.

For the hip-hop producer who had already begun recording funk and soul classics for their rappers to rap over, digital sampling made their work a lot easier and provided new possibilities and ways of making records. Also, most digital sampling drum machines have the capacity of playing a series of samples in a programmed sequence of very complex rhythmic patterns.

Most rap records today incorporate some form of sampling, whether it's the drum sound or an entire section from another record. Among the best examples of sampling in contemporary music today would be any song by Public Enemy, especially "Night of the Living Baseheads," from the album "It Takes a Nation of Millions to Hold us Back."

CAG—1. A very unattractive female. 2. Heroin.

COOP—To pick up a female.

CORE—1. To purchase drugs. 2. Acquire a new girl.

CRATCH—1. Manually manipulating records on a turntable to create an abrasive, percussive sound in tune to the beat. 2. Money.

ENSE—An abbreviation for sensemillia, a very potent strain of marijuana.

ERIOUS—A high form of praise. "The new song by Erik B. and Rakim is real *serious.*"

ERVED, GET—Get beat up.

EVEN DIGITS—A phone number, preferably a female's.

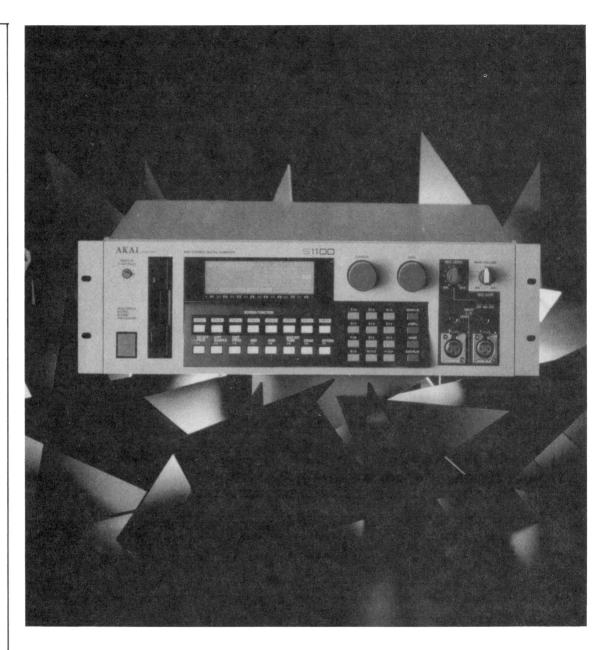

The Akai Digital Sampler, used to make the dopest beats around. *Photo courtesy of AKAI Professional*

2000
TAXPAYERS
RESERVE NOTE
2000
ACC20004KC
ALLEN COUNTY
COUNCIL AT LARGE
THIS NOTE PAID FOR AND AUTHORIZED BY
COMMITTEE TO ELECT KEVIN CAVANAUGH
ALLEN COUNTY COUNCIL AT LARGE
Amanda Cutler
Treasurer of the Committee
CAVANAUGH
SAVE
TAX DOLLARS
VOTE CAVANAUGH
VOTE
ACC20004KC
Kevin Cavanaugh
Will Work Hard For You
2000
2000
TWO THOUSAND

HADES—Sunglasses.

HAKE AND BAKE—To be faked out and scored upon in a basketball game.

HAKE THAT THING—Dance to good black music.

HANK—A knife.

HARP—Well dressed and impressive.

HELL OUT—To pay.

HOOT THE GIFT—To engage in conversation, preferably with a female.

HOW YOU'RE RIGHT—To agree with.

KEEZER—A hip-hop groupie.

KINS—1. Female sex organ. 2. Rolling paper.

KULL—To perform oral sex. This term derives from the popular "head," as in: "He gives the best head ever."

LAMBOYANT—Same as slammin'.

LAMMIN'—1. High form of praise, excellent. 2. Music played loud and proud.

LEEPIN'—Being unaware of things happening around you.

LICK—To obtain your goals in a smooth and possibly unorthodox manner. "The way he got out of paying all those taxes was very *slick."*

LIDE—To move on.

LINGIN'—To sell drugs.

LOB THE KNOB—Oral sex (fellatio).

MOKED, GET—Get killed.

MOKIN'—High form of praise, excellent.

MOOTH—1. An easygoing person or situation. 2. Not harsh to the ear, eye, or touch. "Sade is a **smooth** singer."

MOOTH OPERATOR—One with the ability to effortlessly gain total confidence in women and others.

NAPPIN'—To talk negatively about someone.

OFT—A person easy to take advantage of.

PORT—To wear or have.

QUARE—1. A person unaware of ultra-urban contemporary culture, music, fashion, etc. 2. A cigarette.

QUARE UP—To leave an underground or illegal life style and get a 9 to 5 job.

QUASH—1. To end an ongoing situation. 2. To stop or settle a fight or argument.

TACKED—A well built, curvaceous female.

TALLION—A tall, well-built, curvaceous black female.

TASH—To hide something.

TATIC—Trouble.

TEEL—Firearm.

TEP OFF—To leave.

TEPPIN'—1. To leave. 2. Dance.

TEP TO—To approach someone with the intention of causing trouble. "We

stepped to the suckers who robbed my crib and waxed their asses."

TRAPPED—Carrying a gun.

TRUCK OUT—Male advances on a female and got rejected.

TUNT—Promiscuous female.

TUPID—1. Very. 2. High form of praise as in **stupid** fresh, **stupid** large, or crazy **stupid.**

TUPID, GET—To act wild or crazy and enjoy yourself.

TYLIN' AND PROFILIN'—Being well dressed and flaunting it. (See also **profilin'**.)

UCKER—A person who's easy to push around and take advantage of.

UDS—Beer.

UGAR DADDY—An older man who takes care of a woman's financial or material needs for sexual favors.

WEAT—To bother someone.

YSTEM—Car or home stereo where you blast hip-hop music.

AKE A FALL—1. To lose one's position of prominence. 2. To go to jail.

AKE IT LIGHT—1. Take it easy. 2. A final greeting.

AKE OUT—To kill.

AKING NO SHORTS—1. Not to be taken advantage of. 2. Will not accept less money than something's worth.

ALKING OUT OF THE SIDE OF YOUR NECK—Lying.

APPED OUT—Penniless, broke.

.C.B.—Taking care of business—having sex.

EARING SHIT UP—Performing good music or dance.

ENDERONI—Attractive young female. This word was made popular by a song of the same title by Bobby Brown from his "Don't Be Cruel" LP.

HICK—A shapely, full figured woman.

HROW DOWN—1. To begin a major endeavor. 2. To vigorously dance and party.

HUMPIN'—1. Loud funky music. 2. The sound lots of bass makes.

IP—Way of describing the mood or type of situation you're in or dealing with. "I used to be down with rock but now I'm on the hip-hop *tip*."

Biz Markie, Rap's Clown Prince. *Photo George DuBose. Courtesy of Warner Bros. Records*

VOGUE

O THE CURB—At one's lowest point.

OY—A novice at what they're doing.

RIBE—A group of close friends.

RICK—One who pays for sex.

RIM—Female sex organ.

RIPPIN'—Acting crazy and irrational.

URN IT OUT—1. To have a raucous good time. 2. To display rapping or dancing skills to a crowd's approval.

URN YOU OUT—To introduce to something new.

WELVE HUNDREDS—Technics 1200 turntables. The most preferred by hip-hop D.J.s worldwide for their ability to allow cutting (see definition) and scratching (see definition) at its highest.

WENTY-FOUR/SEVEN/THREE-SIXTY-FIVE—Twenty-four hours a day, seven days a week, and 365 days a year.

LTRA—The highest and the best.

NDER RAPS—Keeping a secret.

ZI—An automatic submachine gun.

APORS, THE—The vibe you give those who only want your friendship because of the notoriety or success you have achieved. Popularized by Biz Markie in a song of the same name.

OGUE—A competitive form of dance developed by New York gays that combines high-fashion modeling gestures with modern dance and acrobatics. Recently popularized by Madonna in her song and video of the same title.

61

ACK—Not good or acceptable.

ASTED—1. Killed. 2. High or intoxicated.

AX—1. A Record. 2. To defeat someone. 3. Have intercourse.

ENT OUT—1. Did something all wrong. 2. Embarrassed yourself when it could have been prevented.

HAT IT BE LIKE?—What's going on?

HAT'S UP WITH THAT?—Explain what you're doing.

HAT TIME IS IT? or **DO YOU KNOW WHAT TIME IT IS?**—Do you know what's happening?

HEELS—Car

HEELS OF STEEL—Two turntables in the hands of a hip-hop D.J.

HOLE NINE YARDS—The whole thing.

IDE OPEN—The point when one falls hopelessly in love. "Now that she's back from Desert Storm, he's totally *wide open.*"

ILD STYLE—1. An elaborate type of graffiti writing. 2. The first film on hip-hop music and culture.

WILD THING, THE—Sexual intercourse, popularized by my lines in Spike Lee's hit film "She's Gotta Have It." " . . . Baby, let's go up to my crib and do the *wild thing . . .* "

WILDIN'—Raucous and rowdy group activity.

WIRED—Too high to go to sleep.

WORD, OR WORD UP—Derived from the phrase "My word is my bond," which means this is not a lie.

WORD TO THE MOTHER—Same as above with more emphasis.

YO—1. Greeting. 2. Title of the first nationally broadcast television rap show. "Yo! MTV Raps." 3. Way of getting someone's attention, as in "*Yo*, what's up?"

YOU ALL THAT—You look good.

YOU CAN'T DO ME NONE—Don't bother me.

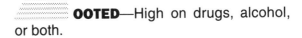

ZERO—A nobody.

ZONKED—Very high on drugs, alcohol, or both.

ZOOTED—High on drugs, alcohol, or both.

This list includes hip hop artists who have recorded and many who have not yet done so.

GROUP	LABEL	RECORD TITLE
ABC		
Above the Law	Epic	Untouchable
A.D.T.		
Afritax Bambaataa	Capitol	Tarzan Boy
		Unity w/James Brown
		Reckless w/UB40
		Shout It Out
		Unity (rapmania)
Afrika Islam		
Afros	JMJ/RAI./Columbia	Feel It
		Kickin Afrolistics
Afro Rican		
AKA Brothers		
Almighty R.S.O. Crew		
Another Bad Creation	Motown	Iesha
		Playground
Antoinette	Next Plateau	Who's The Boss
		Shake, Rattle & Roll
		Never Get Enough
		She Operates Around the Clock
Apache		
Asher D & Daddy Freddy		
Asiatic		
Atmospheric		
Audio 2	1st Priority/Atlantic	I Don't Care
		On The Road Again
		I Get The papers
A Tribe Called Quest		

GROUP	LABEL	RECORD TITLE
Awsome Dre and the Hardcore Committee	Bentley	You Can't Hold Me Back Frankly Speaking
Awsome Threesome	RCA	Nice & Slow
Barsha		
Basic Black		
B D P	Jive/RCA	My Philosophy Jack Of Spades You Must Learn Love's Gonna Get Cha Criminal Minded Why Is That I'm Still #1
Beastie Boys	Def Jam/Columbia	She's On It Fight For Your Right *Hold It Now Hit It* No Sleep Till Brooklyn Hey Ladies Shake Your Rump Shadrach Looking Down The Barrell of Gun
Bell Biv Devoe	MCA	Poison Do Me BBD (Thought It Was Me) She's Dope
B'Fatts	Orpheaus/EMI	Music Maestro
Big Daddy Kane	Cold Chillin'/ Warner Bros.	Ain't No Half Steppin Lean on Me Smooth Operator I Get the Job Done To Be Your Man I Get the Job Done (rapmania) Cause I Can Do It Right All of Me
Big Lady K		

65

GROUP	LABEL	RECORD TITLE
Big Ocean Mob		
Big Pacific		
Biz Markie	Cold Chillin'/ Warner Bros.	Vapors Biz is Goin Off Somethin For The Radio Just A Friend It's Spring Again What Comes Around Goes Around
Bizzie Boys		
Black & White	Atlantic	Feel the Vibe
Black By Demand		Dearly Beloved
Black Radical MK II		
Blackmale		Body Talk
Black, Rock & Ron	RCA	You Can't Do Me None
Black Stallion		
Blondie	Chrysalis	Rapture
Blossom		
Blood Brothers	Jive/RCA	Replica
Bobby Brown		Rock wit' cha
Blvd. Mosse		
B.M.W.F.		
B.M.W.T.		
Bobby, Jimmy & The Critters		Hair or Weave
Bobcat	Arista	I Need You
Body & Soul	Delicious Vinyl/ Island	Dance To The Drummer's Beat
Boi Wundah & The Funkytown Pros		

GROUP	LABEL	RECORD TITLE
Bomb The Bass	Island	Beat Dis
The Boogie Boys	Capitol	I'm Comin
Bootsy's Rubber Band	4th R Broadway	Disciples of Funk
Boo Yaa Tribe	4th & Broadway	R.A.I.D. Psyko Funk
Brand New Heavies		
Brand Nubian	Elektra	Feels So Good Wake Up
Breeze	Atlantic	L.A. Posse Great big Freak
Brenda Fassie		
Brother of the Same Mind		
James Brown	Polydor	Papa's Got A Brand New Bag
Brother 07'		
Brothers For The Struggle		
Brothers Of Soul		
Buffalo Soldiers	Penny	
Buzniss Partners		
Busy Bee	Uni/MCA	Express
B.W.P.	No Face/Ral	We Want Money Wanted
By All Means		Let's Get It On
C & C Music Factory	CBS	Here We Go Lets Rock n Roll
Candyman	Epic	Knockin' Boots Melt In Your Man Nightgown
Captain Kirk		
Captain Rap		

GROUP	LABEL	RECORD TITLE
Captain Rock		
Cash Money & Marvelous		Find An Ugly Woman
Caveman		
CD-3		
C.E.O. And The Senior VP's		
Chad Jackson		
Chapter #3		
Neneh Cherry	Virgin	Buffalo Stance
		Manchild
		Heart
		I've Got You Under My Skin
Cheba	Columbia	The Piper
Chill E. B.		
Chill Rob G.	Wildpitch	The Court Is Now In Session
		The Power
Chilly D.		
Choice		
Chubb Rock	Select	Ya Bad Chubbs
		Treat Em Right
Chuck Brown And The Soul Searchers		The Chubbster
Chuck Chillout & Kool Chip		I'm Large
Chucky A.		Owww!!
Clay D. and the Get Funky Crew		
George Clinton	Capitol	Last Dance
		Atomic Dog
		Why Should I Dog U Out
Cochese		
Cold Crush Brothers		

GROUP	LABEL	RECORD TITLE
Compton's Most Wanted		Growing Up In The Hood
Cold Cuts		
Cookie Crew	FFRR/Polygram	Born This Way
Cool C	Atlantic	Glamorous Life
		Life In The Ghetto
		If You Really Love Me
C.P.O.	Capitol	Ballad Of A Menace
		This Beat Is Funky
Craig G.	Cold Chillin	U R Not The 1
Criminal Nation		
Cut Father		
Cut Master MC		
Cypress Hill Tribe		
Daddy D		
Daddy Freddy	Chrysalis	Daddy Freddy's In Town
D.C. Scorpio		Stone Cold Hustler Part II
Diamond Shell	Cold Chillin	Oh What A Night
D Mob	FFRR/London/ Polygram	It Is Time To Get Funky
		We Called It Acieed
		Glory
D-Nice	Jive/RCA	Call Me D-Nice
		Crumbs On The Table
The D.O.C.	Ruthless/Atlantic	It's Funky Enough
		The D.O.C. And The Doctor
		The Formula
		Beautiful But Deadly
		Mind Blowin'
Dana Dane	Profile	This Be The Def Beat
		A Little Bit of Dane Tonight
		Tales From The Dane Side

GROUP	LABEL	RECORD TITLE
Dangerous Dame		
Danny D. And DJ Wiz		
Daughter Brite And The Soda Pop Mikes		
Dave Tech N-Ice		
Davey D		
Davey DMX		
D-Breeze		
Deep State 2		
Def Casper		
Def City		
Def Games	Sedona	Set It Off
Def Duo		
Definition Of Sound		Now Is Tomorrow
Def IV		
Def Jef	Delicious Vinyl	Give It Here
		Droppin' Rhymes On Drums
		Black To The Future
Def 2 The Flesh etc		
Defiant Giants		
De La Soul	Tommy Boy	Potholes In My Lawy
		Me, Myself And I
		Say No Go
		Buddy
		Ring Ring Ring
		Ring Ring Ring (Unplugged)
		Saturday
Demon Boiz		

GROUP	LABEL	RECORD TITLE
Derek B	Profile	We've Got The Juice Bad Young Brother We've Got The Juice
Derek K		
Deskee		
Deuces Wild		
Diane Brown and Barry K. Sharp		
Digital Underground	Tommy Boy	Doowatchyalike The Humpty Dance Doowatchyalike (V.II) Same Song
Disco Rick And The Boys		
Dis Master		
Divine Force		
Divine Sound		
Divine Styler		
DJ Chuck Chillout	Mercury/Polygram	Rhythm Is The Master
DJ Aladdin		
DJ Double J		
DJ HD		
DJ Jazzy Jeff & Fresh Prince	Jive/RCA	Parents Just Don't Understand Girls Ain't Nothing But Trouble Brand New Funk I Think I Can Beat Mike Tyson Summertime
DJ Mark And The 45 Kings		
DJ Mark with LaKim		
DJ Marley Marl		
DJ Pierre		

GROUP	LABEL	RECORD TITLE
DJ Pike		
DJ Quick	Profile	Born And Raised In Compton Tonite
DJ Skill		
Divine Styler	Feat The Scheme Teen	Ain't Saying Nothing
D-Money		
D.M.I.	Dirty Mina Inc.	
D.N.A.		
D.Nice		
Doc Box & B Fresh		
Doctor Groove		
Doctor Ice	Jive/RCA	Word To The Wise
Donald D		FBI Notorious?
Double D. & Steinski		
Double T And The Downtown Posse	Next Plateau	Owner Of A Broken Heart
Doug E. Fresh	Danya/Reality	Keep Risin To The Top All The Way To Heaven Cut That Zero D E F = Dough F Fresh Summertime
Doug Lazy	Atlantic	Can't Hold Back
Downtown Science	Def Jam	Radioactive Room To Breathe
Dr. Dré		
Mickey Dread		Source Of Your Divorce
Dream Warriors	4th & B'Way	Wash Your Face In My Sink My Defimition Of A.... Bombastic Jazz Style

GROUP	LABEL	RECORD TITLE
Dr. Jam		
Dr. Jekyll & Mr. Hyde		
D.R. & The Bague Crew		
D Shake		
DST		
D Style		
Drum	4th & B'way	Swirl
Dutchezz		
Earle The Poet	EMI	High Noon
Eazy E	Priority	We Want Easy
		Easy-er Said Than Dunn
Ebony Lover & DJ Cra-z Jaye	Cold Front	Slippin'
ECD		
E.C.P.	Emerald City Possee	
Ed O.G. & Da Bulldogs	PWL/Mercury	I Got To Have It
		Bug A Boo
Eerk & Jerk		Eerk & Jerk
Elements of Style		
En Touch		
Epic		
EPMD	Sleeping Bag/Fresh	Strickly Business
		You Got To Chill
		So What Cha Sayin'
		You Had Too Much To Drink
		Golddigger
		Rampage
		Got To Give The People
Eric & Blow Torch & The Force Of Victory		

GROUP	LABEL	RECORD TITLE
Eric B & Rakim	4th & Broadway UNI/MCA	Paid In Full Move The Crowd (Island) Follow The Leader Microphone Friend Let The Rhythm Hit'em Let The Rhythm Hit'em (Live) In The Ghetto
E-Roc c-c		
Euro K	Profile	She's A . . .
Eveready & Smoovie		
Everlast	Warner Bros.	Syndication I Got The Knack The Rhythm
Face Down		
Fantasy Three		
Fascinating Force		
Fast Eddie		
Fat Back		
Fat Boys	Tin Pan/Polygram	Can You Feel It Sex Machine Wipe Out The Twist Are You Ready For Freddy Louie, Louie Lie-Z
Father MC	Uptown/MCA	Treat Them Like They Want To Be Treated I'll Do 4 U Lisa Baby
F.B.I.		
Fearless 4		

GROUP	LABEL	RECORD TITLE
Fifth Platoon	SBK	Party Line
Final Call		
Final Conflict		
Finesse & Synquis	MCA	Soul Sisters
		Straight From The Soul
Flavor-Flar		
Force MD's		
49ers		
Foster & McElroy		
Freak L		
Freddie Foxxx		
Freshco & Miz	Tommy Boy	We Don't Play
Full Effect		
Full Force		Ain't My Type Of Hype
Funkadelic		
Funk Mafia		
Funky Alien		
Furious Five		
Future		
Gang Starr Posse		
Gary Byrd & The GBE		
Genuine Posse		
George Clinton		
Gerardo		Rico Suave
		We Want The Funk
Geto Boys		Do It Like A G.O.

GROUP	LABEL	RECORD TITLE
Gizmo		
Globe & Whiz Kid		
Grand Daddy I.U.	Cold Chillin	Something New
Grandmaster Caz		
Grandmaster Flash	Elektra	U Know What Time It Is
		The Message (Sugar Hill)
Grandmaster Melle Mel		
Grandmaster Slice		
Grege		
Grove B Chill	A&M	Hip Hop Music
Gucci		
Gucci Crew II	Gucci	Pushin
Gunshot		
Hard Noise		
Harmony	Virgin	Poundcake
Heavy D & The Boyz	Uptown/MCA	Overweight Lovers
		We Got Our Own Thang
		Some Body For Me
		Gyrlz They Love Me
		Now That We Found Love
Henry G		
HI-C		
High Performance	Nastymix	Do You Really Wanna Party
		All Things Considered
		It's Just Funky
Hijack		
Hip House Syndicate		Free James Brown

GROUP	LABEL	RECORD TITLE
Hi Tec 3		
Howie Tee		
Hugh E. MC & DJ-XI		
Hurricane		Over The Edge
H.W.A.		Hoes With Attitudes
Ice Cold Mode		
Ice Cream Tee	MCA	Let's Work
Ice Cube	Priority	Who's The Mack
		Dead Homiez
		Jackin' For Beats
Ice Man		
Ice MC	Chrysalis	Easy
Ice-T	Sire	Colors
		I'm Your Pusher
		High Rollers
		Lethal Weapon
		You Played Yourself
		What Ya Wanna Do
		New Jack Hustler
		O.G. Original Ganster
Icey Jaye		It's A Girl Thing
Ihzan		
Information Society		
Intelligent Hoodlum	A&M	Black & Proud
		Black To Reality
		Arrest The President
Iron Mike & J Kool		
Isaac Hayes		
Isadore		

GROUP	LABEL	RECORD TITLE
Isis	4th & B'way	Rebel Soul The Power Of Myself Is... Moving
Chad Jackson		Hear The Drummer (Get Wicked)
Jaz	EMI	Hawaiian Sophie The Originators A Groove (This Is What U)
Jazzi & Neat		
Jazzy Joyce		
J.C. Lodge		
Jesse West		
Jibri Wise One		The House The Dog Built
Jimmy Spicer		
J.J. Fad	Atco/Atlantic	Supersonic Is It Love We In The House Be Good Ta Me
Joeski Love	Columbia	Peewee's Dance I Know She Likes Joe Joe Cool
Joey B. Ellis	Capitol	Go For It Go For It Thought U Were The One... For Me
Joey Kid		
J.T.		Swing It
Juice Crew		
Jungle Brothers	Warlock	I'll House You Straight Out Of The Jungle Beyond This World

GROUP	LABEL	RECORD TITLE
		What U Waitin' For
		Doin' Our Own Dang
		I Get A Kick Out Of You
Junkyard Band		
Just Ice	Sleeping Bag/Fresh	Goin Way Back
		Welfare Recipient
JVC Force		
Kash Da Masta		
K Cloud And The Crew		
K.C. Flight	RCA	Planet E
KMD	Elektra	Peach Fuzz
		Who Me
K.M.C. Kru		She's My Cutie
K-9 Posse	Arista	Ain't Nothing To It
		This Beat Is Military
K-Solo	Atlantic	Spellbound
		Your Mom's In My Business
		Fugitive
K-Yze		Stomp (Jump Move Your Body)
Kid Crab		
Kid Capri		Appollo
Kid Frost	Virgin	La Raza
		La Raza (v.II)
		That's It (Ya Estuvo)
Kid Jam		
Kid-&-Play	Select/Warner Bros.	Do This My Way
		Gittin Funky
		Rollin With Kid n Play
		Too Hype
		Funhouse

79

GROUP	LABEL	RECORD TITLE
		Back To Basix
		Ene'gy
Kid Sensation	Nastymix	Seatown Ballers
		Prisioner Of Ignorance
King Bee		
King MC		
King Of Chill		
Kings Of Pressure	Next Plateau	Tales From The Darkside
Kings Of Swing	Virgin	Nod Your Head To This
		U Know I Love Ya Baby
King Sun	Profile	On The Club Tip
		It's A Heat Up
		Be Black
		Undercover Lover
King Tee	Capitol	Bass
		Ruff Rhyme
		Diss You
		At Your Own Risk
Kokaine		
Kool Chip		
Kool DJ Here		
Kool DJ Red Alert		
Kool Gee Rap & DJ Polo	Cold Chillin	Road To The Riches
		Streets Of New Your
		Erase Racism
Kool Moe Dee	Jive/RCA	Wild Wild West
		How You Like Me Now
		They Want Money
		I Go To Work
		All Night Long
		God Made Me Funke

GROUP	LABEL	RECORD TITLE
		Rise And Shine
		How Kool Can A Blackman Be
Kool Stool	Capitol	My Girl
		U Can't Buy My Love
Kozmo Flex		
K-Rob		
Krown Rules		
KRS-One		
Krush Groove	Warner Bros.	Kursh Groovin
K-Solo		
K-Swift		
Kurtis Blow	Polygram	Don't You Love America
		Basketball
		U Gotz To Get Down
Kwame	Atlantic	The Man We All Know And Love
		The Rhythm
		U Gotz 2 Get Down
		Ownlee Ewe
		Oneovdabigboiz
Kyze		
Patti Labelle		Yo Mister
LA Dream Team		
Lady Fresh		
Lady Levi	Motown	Looking For A Dope Beat
Lady Love		
Lakim Shabazz	Tuff City	Black Is Back
		Pure Righteousness
		The Lost Tribe Of Shabazz
		Need Some Lovin'
La Luv		

GROUP	LABEL	RECORD TITLE
Lano Of Confusion		
Laquan	4th & B'way	Now's The B-Turn
		Swing Blue, Sweat Black
Larry Larr		Larry, That's What They...
		Call Me
La Star	Profile	Fade To Black
		Swing To The Beat
L'Trim	Atlantic	Cars That Go Boom
Latin Empire		
L.A. Posse	Atlantic	Countdown
Leaders/New School	Elektra	Case Of The PTA
		Sobb Story
Leather Cap Posse (.L.C.P.)		
Legion Of Doom		
Leita K		
Le Juan Love		
Levert	Atlantic	Just Coolin
Barrington Levy		Here I Come
Profile		
Living Color Freaturing Daddy O		Funny Vibe
LL Cool J	Def Jam/Columbia	Goin Back To Cali
		I'm Bad
		I Need Love
		I'm That Type Of Guy
		Big Ole Butt
		One Shot At Love
		Jingling Baby
		Boomin' System
		Round The Way Girl
		Mama Said Knock U Out
		Mama Said Knock U Out v.2

GROUP	LABEL	RECORD TITLE
		Mama Said Knock U Out (club)
		Jingling Baby
		Mama Said Knock U Out (Unpl)
Lord Finess & DJ Smooth	Wildpitch	Strickly For The Ladies
Low Profile	Priority	Funky Song
Luke F/2 Live Crew		Banned In The USA
		Mama Juanita
Maceo & Fred Wesley		
Maestro Fresh-Wes		Let Your Backbone Slide
		Drop The Needle
M.A.F.I.A.		
Main Source	Actual	"Watch Roger Do His Thing"
		Looking At The Front Door
		Just Hangin' Out
Malcolm McClaren	Island	Buffalo Gals
		Double Dutch
		Duck For The Ousters
Mamado & She	Wig	Can We Take You Higher
Mantronix	Capitol	Join Me Please
		Simple Simon
Many Fazes	Big Beat	I'm Hip
Mark Dee	MCA	Get A Hold Of Yourself
Markey Fresh		
Bob Marley	Tuff Gang/Island	Could You Be Loved
		One Love
		Redemption Song
		Waiting In Vain
		Buffalo Soldier
		Buffalo Soldier
		Get Up Stand Up
		I Shot The Sheriff

GROUP	LABEL	RECORD TITLE
Rita & Stephen Marley		Who Colt The Game
Ziggy Marley	Virgin	Black My Story Not History
		Look Who's Dancing
		Tumblin' Down
		All Love
		One Bright Day
		What's True
		Tomorrow People
Marly Marl	Cold Chillin'/ Warner Bros.	Symphony
Master Ace	Cold Chillin/ Reprise	Me & The Biz
		Music Man
Master Don Committee		
Master Gee		
Master O.C. & Crazy Eddie		
Master Of The Ceremony		
Master P		
Maxi Priest		
Curtis Mayfield & Ice T.		Superfly 1990
MBS Transmit Power		
MC Ade		
MC Antdog & DJ Gamble		
MC Breeze		
MC Chase		
MC Coolie		
MC Downbeat		
M.C. Hammer	Island	Let's Get It Started
		Pump It Up
		Turn This Mutha Out
		They Put Me In The Mix

GROUP	LABEL	RECORD TITLE
		Dancin' Machine
		Help The Children
		U Can't Touch This
		Have You Seen Her
		Pray
		Here Comes The Hammer
		Here Comes The Hammer
Malcolm Mclaren	Island	Buffalo Gals
		Double Dutch
		Duck For The Oysters
MBS		Transmit Power
MC J-Cove G		
MC Joy & DJ Villan		
MC Lyte	1st Priority/ Atlantic	Paper Thin
		Lyte As A Rock
		I'm Not Having It
		Cha, Cha, Cha
		Stop, Look, & Listen
		Cappucino
		Cappucino (Unplugged Ver.)
MC Rell & The House Rockers	Mercury/Polygram	Into The Future
		Life Of An Entertainer
MC Ren		
MC Richie Rich & Scratch		
MC Rumble		
MC Sergio	Idlers	In The Name Of Love
MC Shan	Cold Chillin'/ Warner Bros.	Left Me Lonely
		Don't Mean A Thing
		Its Time To Defend Ourselves
MC Shy D	On Top	Shake It
		Don't Sweat Me
MC Smooth	Crush Music	Smooth and Legit

GROUP	LABEL	RECORD TITLE
		You Gotta Be Real
		Where Is The Money
MC Supreme	Warner Bros.	Black In America
MC Trouble f/Good Girls	Motown	I Wanna Make You Mine
		Gotta Get A Grip
MC Twist & The Def Squad	Skywalker	Shock The House
Melle Mel	Sugar Hill	Pump Me Up
		The Message
		What's The Matter With My World
Mello Man Ace	Capital	Rhyme Fighter
		Mentirosa
Melon		
Miami Boyz	On Top	I Am Ready To Go
Miami Style Posse		
Michael Concepcion		
Michie Mae And L.A.	First Priority	Jamaica Funk
Monie Love	Warner Bros.	Monie In The Middle
		It's A Shame
Mr. Lee	Jive/RCA	Get Busy
		Pump That Body
		I Like The Girls
Ms. Melodie		Live On Stage
Naughty By Nature	Tommy Boy	O.P.P.
N.W.A.	Priority	Express Yourself
		100 Miles & Runnin'
Nemesis	Profile	I Want Your Sex
Next School		Profits Of Unity
Nice & Smooth	Fresh	Early To Rise
		Funky For You

GROUP	LABEL	RECORD TITLE
Nikki D	Def Jam/CBS	Letting Off Steam Daddy's Little Girl Hang On Kid
No Face	Jam/Ral/Columbia	Half Fake Hair Wearing
Nu Sounds	Strong City/Uni/MCA	Condition Red Body Slam
Oaktowns 357	Capitol	Yeah Yeah Yeah Straight At You Juicy Gotcha Crazy We Like It
Officer And A Gentleman		Work The House
One Cause, One Effect	Bust It/Capitol	Up With Hope, Down With Dope
Operation Dope		
Organized Crime Unit		
Origanized Confusion		Who Stole My Last Piece Of
Oran"Juice" Jores	Def Jam/Columbia	Here I Go Again
Original Concept		
Overord X Posse		
Papa San	Pow Wow	New Dance Dancehall Good To Me
Paris	Tommy Boy	Break The Grip Of Shame
Parliament		
Partners In Kryme		Undercover
Party Posee		
Party Rican		
Paula Brion		
P.C.P.	People's Choice Possee	
P.C.P.	Prison City Possee	

GROUP	LABEL	RECORD TITLE
Peaches		
Phase N'Rhythm		Swollen Pockets
P.H.D.		
Poison Clan	Luke Records	Dance All Night
Poor Righteous Teachers	Profile	Rock Dis Funky Joint
		Holy Intellect
Positively Black		Escape From Reality
Power Rule		Smooth
		Brick In A Wall
Precious	Big Beat	Definitions Of A Track On Motion
		Let's Get It Started
P.R.E.C.I.S.E. M.C.		All Night Thang
Professor Griff	Skywalker	Pawn In The Game
		The Verdict
Professor X	Island	What's Up G?
Project X		
Public Enemy	Def Jam/Columbia	Night Of The Living Baseheads
		Rebel Without A Pause
		Black Steel In The Hour Of Chaos
		Fight The Power (Perf.)
		Don't Believe The Hype
		Night Of The Lining Basehead
		Welcome To The Terrordome
		911 Is A Joke
		Rebel Without A Pause
		Brothers Gonna Work It Out
		Burn Hollywood Burn
		Terminator X Buck Whylin
Pumpkin & The All Stars		
Q.D. III Soundlab	F/Justin Warfield	Season Of The Vic

GROUP	LABEL	RECORD TITLE
Queen Mother Rage		Slipping Into Darkness
Queen Latifah	Tommy Boy	Dance 4 Me
		Ladies First
		Come Into My House
Quick G		
Quincy Jones		I'll Be good To You
Colin Quinn		Going Back To Brooklyn
Raheem	A&M	Dance Floor
Rakhim		
Randy Mac		
Rappin Is Fundamental	A&M	Rapping Is Fundamental
The Real Roxanne	Select/Warner Bros.	Respect
		Roxanne's On A Roll
The Rebel MC And Double Trouble		Street Tuff
		Rebel Music
Red Bandit F/Ricky Bell	Motown	Please Don't Cry
Readhead Kingpins	Virgin	Do The Right Thing
		Pump It Hottie
		We Rock The Mic Right
		We Don't Have A Plan B
		Get It Together
		It's A Love Thang
Rich Nice	Motown	The Rhythm, The Feeling
		Outstanding
Rob Base & DJ E-Z Rock		It Takes Two
		Get On The Dance Floor
		Joy & Pain
		Times Are Getting Ill
		Turn It Out (Go Base)
		Get Up & Have A Good Time
		Outstanding

GROUP	LABEL	RECORD TITLE
Rock N Gee & DJ Shawn		Swing Beat
Rodney O-Joe Cooley	Atlantic	Say It Loud
		Hocus Pocus
		Get Ready To Roll
Ron C	Profile	Do Dat Danz
Roxanne Shante	Cold Chillin'/	Roxanne's Revenge
	Warner Bros.	Wack It
		Live On Stage
Run DMC	Profile	King Of Rock
		Rockbox
		Walk This Way
		It's Tricky
		Christmas In Hollis
		Run's House
		Mary Mary #1
		I'm Going Out Like That
		Ghostbusters Rap
		Pause
		The Ave.
		The Ave. (long version)
		What's It All About
		Walk This Way
		It's Tricky
		King Of Rock
		Faces
Ruthless Rap Assassins		
Salt-N-Pepa	Next Plateau	Push It
		Shake Your Thang
		Tramp
		Everybody Get Up
		Twist And Shout
		Expression
		Expression (Brixton remix)
		Independent
		Do You Want Me

GROUP	LABEL	RECORD TITLE
Schoolly D	Jive/RCA	Do You Want Me (U.K. remix)
		Let's Talk About Sex
		No More Rock N Roll
		Living In A Jungle
		King Of NY
Scott La Rock	Second Power	
Tony D	Strong City	Check The Elevation
Tony Scott		Get Into It
Serious Lee Fine		Nothing Can Stop Us
7A3	Geffen	Goes Like Dis
		Let The Bells Ring
Shabba Ranks	Epic	Trailer Load A Girls
Shanta		
Shazzy	Elektra	Keep It Flowin'
		Giggahoe
Shelly Thunder		
Shinehead	Elektra	Chain Gang Rap
		Gimme No Crack
		Chain Gang Rap "Live"
		Family Affair
		The Real Rock
Shocky Shay		
Shut Up & Dance		
Sid & B. Tonn		Deathwish
Side F-X	Nastymix	Rock The House
Silk Tymes Leather	Geffen	Do Your Dance (Work It Out)
		The Woman In Me
Sir Mix-A-Lot	Nastymix Records	Posse On Broadway
		Beepers
		My Hooptie

GROUP	LABEL	RECORD TITLE
Skinny Boys	Jive/RCA	They Can't Get Enough
Slammin' Syndicate		
Slick Rick	Def Jam/Columbia	Teenage Love
		Children Story
		Hey Young World
		I Shouldn't Have Done It
Slim & The Secret Society	Posse	Everybody (On The Floor)
Sly & Robbie	Island	Dance Hall
Smooth Ice	JDK	Do It Again
		Smooth But Def
Smooth Mello Rock 24-7		
Snap		The Power
Son Of Bazerk	S.O.U.L./MCA	Change The Style
		Band Gets Swivey
Soula	Warner Bros.	Soul Sister
Soul Kings		
Soul Mate		
Soul Shock		
Soul Sista		
Soul Sonic Force	Tommy Boy	Renegades Of Funk
Soul II Soul	Virgin	Keep On Movin
		Jazzie's Groove
		Back To Live
		Get A Life
Sparky D		
Special Ed	Profile	I Got It Made
		Think About It
		I'm The Magnificent
		The Mission
		Come On Lets Move It
		Girl's Gonna Getcha

GROUP	LABEL	RECORD TITLE
Special F/X		
Spoonie Gee		
Sprint Crew		
Steady B	Zomba/RCA	Serious Nasty Girls Going Steady Girl's Gonna Getcha
Stereo MC		
Steinski & Mass Media	4th & B'way/Island	We'll Be Right Back
Stereo MC's	4th & B'way/Island	Elevate My Mind
Stetsasonic	Tommy Boy	A.F.R.I.C.A. Talkin All That Jazz Speaking Of A Girl Named Suzy A.F.R.I.C.A. (V.I.) No B.S. Allowed
Stevie B	JMR	In My Eyes
Stezo	Fresh Record/ Sleeping Bag	It's My Turn Freak The Funk
Stop The Violence Movement	Jive/RCA	Self Destruction
Style	Select	What A Brother Know Assassinator Who Do You Love
Sugerhill Gang	Sugarhill	Rappers Delight Eight Wonders Rapper's Delight (rapmania)
Super Lover Cee & Cassanova Rud	Elektra	Girls I Got Em Locked
Surf MC's	Profile	Surf Or Die
Sweet Tee	Profile	On The Smooth Tip Why Dit It Have To Be Me

GROUP	LABEL	RECORD TITLE
Terminator X	Def Jam	Buck Whylin Homey Don't Play Dat
3rd Bass	Columbia/Def Jam	Steppin' To The A.M. Gas Face Brooklyn-Queens Triple Stage of Darkness Product Of The Environment Pop Goes The Weasel
Three Times Dope	Arista	Greatest Man Alive Funky Dividends Weak At The Knees
Throw Down Twins		You'll Be On It
Shelly Thunder	Island	Break Up Working Girl
Tone Loc	Delicious Vinyl/Island	Funky Cold Medina Wild Thing I Got It Goin' On
Tony Rock		Street Resident
Tony Toni Rone	Wing/Polygram	Oakland Stroke Feels Good The Blues
Too Nice	Arista	Pop Song 89 I Get Minze
Too Poetic	Tommy Boy	Got Made Me Funky For Those Who Like To Groove
Too Short	Jive/RCA	Life Is Too Short I Ain't Trippin Ghetto Short But Funky
A Tribe Called Quest	Jive/RCA	I Left My Wallet In El Segundo Bonita Applebum Can I Kick It Can I Kick It (Unplugged)
Tuff Crew		Robinhood

GROUP	LABEL	RECORD TITLE
Twin Hype	Profile	Do It To The Crowd For Those Who Like To Groove Nothing Could Save Ya
24-7 Spyz	Relativity	Jungle Boogie
2 Live Crew	Luke Skywalker	Move Something Do Wah Ditty Yakkety Yak Me So Horny
2 Bigg MC	Crush	He's All The Way Live
Tyrone Brunson	Epic	Fresh
The U.B.C.	EMI	U.B. Style
The U Krew	Enigma	If U Were Mine
Ultra Magnetic	Next Plateau	Traveling At The Speed Of Thought
Unity 2		Shirley What Is It, Yo?! Buckwheat The Rebel
Uptown		
Urban Dance Squad	Arista	No Kid (Acoustic Vers)
UTFO	Select/Warner Bros.	Roxanne, Roxanne Leader Of The Pack
UZI Brothers		Nothing But A Gangster
Vanilla Boys		
Vanilla Ice	SBK	Ice Ice Baby Play That Funky Music
Vicious Base F/DJ Magic Mike	Cheetah	It's Automatic
Vicious Beat Posse		Give The People What...
Vicious Trouble		
Jodie Whatley With Eric B. & Rakim	MCA	Friends
Wee Papa Girl Rappers	Jive/RCA	Heat It Up Wee Rule

GROUP	LABEL	RECORD TITLE
West Coast Rap All Stars	Warner Bros.	We're All In The Same We're All In The Same Gang
Whiz Kid With YSL		
Whodini	Jive/RCA	Be Yourself Big Mouth Funky Beat Rock You Again When The Freaks Come Out At Night One Love Any Way I Gotta Swing It Freaks
Winans F/Teddy Riley	Reprise	It's Time
W.I.Z.E. Guyz		Time For Peace
Wrecks n Effects		Let's Do It Again New Jack Swing
X Clan		Heed The Word Of The Brother Funkin' Lesson
Young Black Teenagers	S.O.U.L./MCA	Nobody Knows Kelli Loud & Hard To Hit
Young M.C.	4th & B'way	Bust A Move I Come Off I Come Off (rapmania) Pick Up The Pace That's The Way Love Goes
Young & Restless		B'Girls
Yo-Yo	East West Records	Stompin' To Tha 90's You Can't Play w/My Yo-Yo Ain't Nobody Better
YZ (Anthony Hill)		Tower With The Power Thinking Of A Master Plan Who's That Girl On Our Own Every Little Step